To CJ
Thank you for making the best lemonade day or night and sharing your secret recipe so I could learn to make my own.

First Published in 2024 by Honey Nook Publishing

ISBN 978-1-0369-0842-3

LEMONADE STAND

This book belongs to
Chief Lemonader:
____

When life gives you lemons...

You make...
LEMONADE

Juggle and juice

LEMONADE
making the most of every lemon
for its bright and juicy use

When life gives you lemons...

You make...
LEMONADE

Everyday brings new adventures to explore

You may find some easy

while some may be hard

but with curiosity and patience

you will surely go far!

When life gives you lemons...

You make...
Lemonade

It's a little bit sweet

and a little bit sour

When mixed just right
shake
shake
shake
shake
shaken
stirred
stir
stir
stir
in your own special way

you will find...

Its a
SUPERPOWER

When life gives you lemons...

and you've made
LEMONADE

Be sure to share
You never know whose day you'll brighten...

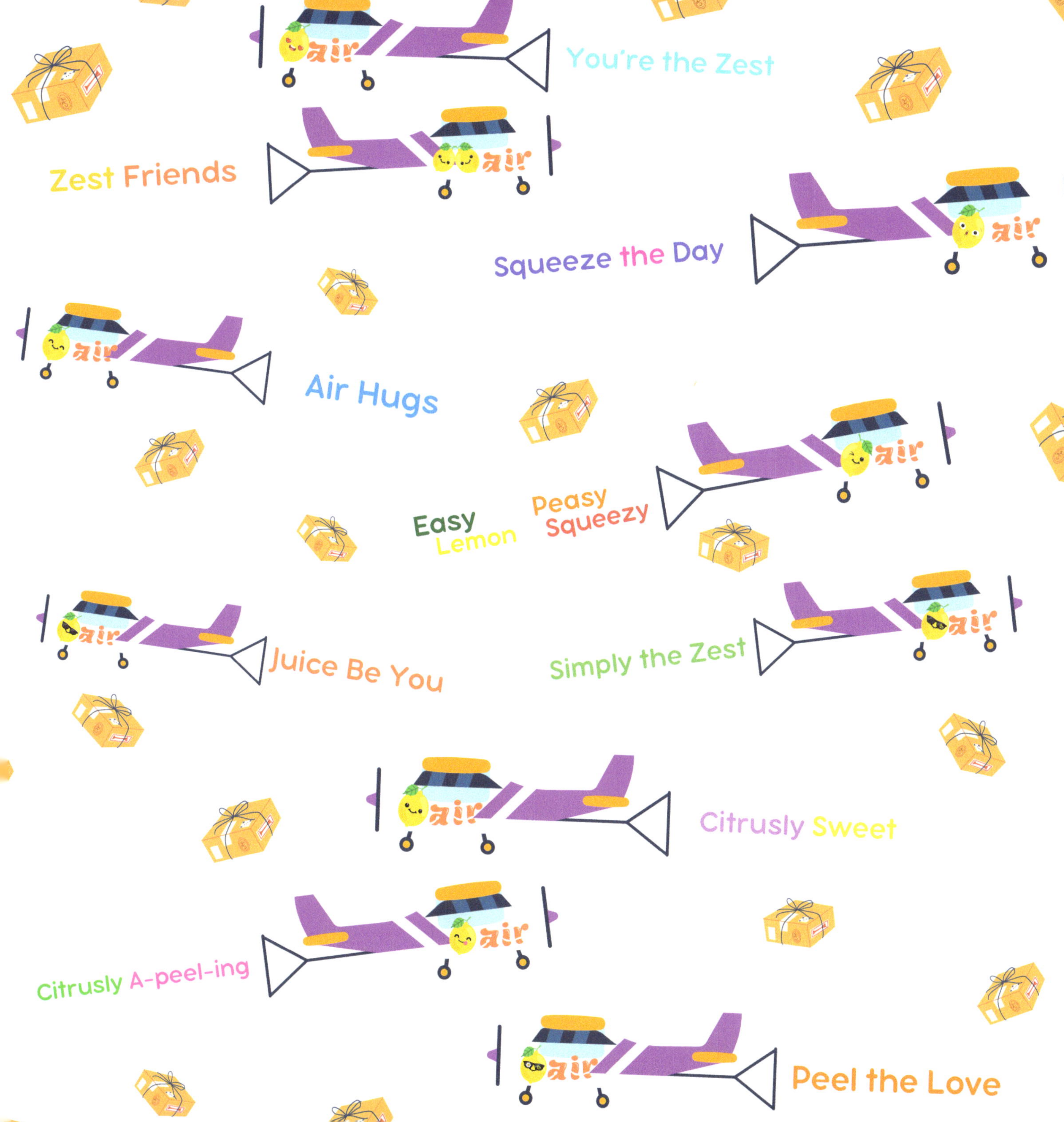

You're the Zest
Zest Friends
Squeeze the Day
Air Hugs
Easy Lemon Peasy Squeezy
Juice Be You
Simply the Zest
Citrusly Sweet
Citrusly A-peel-ing
Peel the Love

Remember

Lemonade is better shared!

(*Just like life*)

A word by the author
Your voice truly matters.
So if you enjoyed this book it would mean the world to me you would take a short minute to share a review on Amazon or your purchasing website.

Your kind feedback is very much appreciated & very important. Thank you so much for your time.

May your life be as delightfully balanced as the perfect glass of lemonade.

www.ingramcontent.com/pod-product-compliance
Lightning Source LLC
Chambersburg PA
CBHW042142030726
47599CB00002B/587